Remarkable Names
of Real People
or
How to Name Your Baby

Karen Sherve

Hugh Pugh, Landscape Architect, London

Remarkable Names
of Real People

or

How to Name Your Baby

Compiled & annotated by
John Train

Illustrations by Pierre Le-Tan
Introduction by S. J. Perelman

Clarkson N. Potter, Inc., Publishers, New York
Distributed by Crown Publishers, Inc.

Published simultaneously in Canada by General Publishing Company Limited
First edition
Printed in the United States of America

The portraits in this book are drawn entirely from my imagination and are in no way intended to be considered as likenesses or caricatures of the people named.

—Pierre Le-Tan

An earlier version of this book appeared in the Paris Review *under the title* How to Name Your Baby.

Designed by Katy Homans
Type set in Monotype Dante by Michael & Winifred Bixler

Library of Congress Cataloging in Publication Data

Train, John.
    Remarkable names of real people.

    A new and expanded ed. of a booklet published privately in 1972 under title: How to name your baby.
    1. Names, Personal—Anecdotes, facetiae, satire, etc. I. Title.
ISBN 0-517-531305 (cloth)
      0-517-543036 (paper)

10 9 8 7 6

ACKNOWLEDGMENTS

The Office of Nomenclature Stabilization is grateful to its many faithful correspondents in the United States and abroad, starting with Joseph Fox, our collaborator for many years. Others are Timothy Dickinson, Margaret Bishop, her cousin Charles Harding and her brother Judge Don Young, George Plimpton, Candida Donadio, Robert Myrhum, Jennifer Raper, Frances Fosburgh, Peter Matthiessen, Nina Georges-Picot, S. J. Perelman, Brendan Gill, Alan Pryce-Jones, Jack Baumgarten, Howard Irwin, Clement Wood, Shelby Cullom Davis, Jerry Goodman, Pembroke Hart, Ormonde de Kay, Peter Thacher, Francine Lefrak, Robert Haynes, Fayette Hickox, Piers Dixon, Axie Whitney, Christopher Mallaby, Mrs. Doyle Klyn, Patricia Polak, Granya Gurevich, Kay Leperq, Richard Lamb, Leroy Morgan, Charles Chatfield, Joy Dineen, and Professors William Grierson, Howard Mumford Jones, Richard Gregg, Leonard Ashley, and Michael Coe. To the many whose diligence has not yet resulted in a verified entry, persevere! Those seriously interested in names should examine Percy H. Reaney's remarkable Origin of English Surnames. *The Pliny of American onomastics was the indefatigable H. L. Mencken, to whom this little work is respectfully dedicated.*

Concerto Macaroni

PREFACE

Earlier this year, soon after the Indian electorate swept
Indira Gandhi into the dustbin, a lady novelist named Lois
Gould wrote a purportedly satiric piece for the New York
Times. Evidently her ire had been aroused by the statement
of Morarji Desai, the new prime minister: "When a woman becomes devilish, she beats all the records. Now I can't
say that she [Mrs. Gandhi] is all devil . . . but the good is
suppressed and the devil is on top." Infuriated that Desai
had thus kicked feminism in the groin, Miss Gould seized on
comedy as an effective weapon to demolish him, and she con-
jectured three personalities for her lampoon—Dr. J. S.
Mindblow of Harvard, Dr. R. V. Doppelgang of Yale, and
a Dr. Tatiana Moxie, academic connection unspecified. The
second I read these names, the Times fell from my nerveless
hand and I was overcome by the mixture of neuralgia and
depression that parlor comedians always induce in their
auditors. That the fair columnist was as funny as a cry on
the moors was instantly apparent, but I forced myself to
finish her piece, and my suspicion was corroborated. As a
novelist Miss Gould is doubtless superlative; I have yet to
find out. As a wag, she had waded beyond her depth.

What bearing, you may properly ask, has the forego-
ing on the present work? The answer is that try as it will,
Art can never hope to surpass reality, and in assembling

this gallimaufry of actual names, the industrious Mr. Train has ransacked Nature to confirm the extraordinary riches of the world around us.

The people listed herein, let it be emphasized, are not fictional characters laboriously devised by the sophomoric to tickle the funny bone. They are real individuals, afflicted like the rest of us with bunions, flatulence, and presbyopia; folk who consult daily horoscopes, shlep their wetwash to the laundromat, fret about their sagging busts or their potency, and survive—God knows how—under the burden their parents have laid on them at the baptismal font. And because they do exist, they excite a dual response in the reader—an astonishment so vast that he dissolves into laughter, coupled with relief that his own name is pedestrian. That is, unless he is an Armenian named Pedestrian, in which case his gratification subsides like a toy balloon.

Along with the bizarrerie in these pages, however, it is worthy of note that very many of the names included have a distinct poetic or lyrical rhythm, and I can well imagine chanting oneself to sleep by repeating Suparporn Poopattana and Sistine Madonna McClung. I note with regret that the chronicler has seen fit to omit a heroine of my youth, Ming Toy Epstein, whose name had the sweet, tinkling purity of temple bells. He has, likewise, neglected to commemorate one Dolores del Schultz whom Dashiell Hammett once disclosed he met while a Pinkerton operative in San Francisco. As is inevitable in all works of scholarship, there are trifling minor errors; Toilet Jacobs was not a student at the Minneapolis School of Art but rather, as Lillian Hellman assured me, a schoolfellow of hers in New York.

8

Nonetheless, in culling such fragrant blooms from the files of newspapers, magazines, and educational institutions, Train and his network of informants have followed a great tradition. We know that Dickens' researches in the press and street directories of his day gave us immortalia like Dombey and Chuzzlewit, Podsnap, Uriah Heep, and Sairey Gamp—names resonant with authenticity, blessedly free of scamp-of-the-campus cuteness. Perhaps this collection will serve both as a reference work and a stimulus to others in the literary dodge to do the same.

—S. J. Perelman

Goody P. Creep, Undertaker

How to Name Your Baby

Too often well-intentioned parents, for lack of professional guidance, give their children names that stifle the infant's individuality. Psychologists remind us that an inappropriate name may affect a child's character: a dull name can mean a dull child. This guide is therefore offered to perplexed parents to suggest some possibilities they might not otherwise have considered. All of them are real names of real persons.

As most people know instinctively, there is a curious magic in names. If you call your little one Elmer *he is less likely to amount to anything than if you plunge in with a* Charlemagne *or a* Napoleon. *(Had the Emperor been christened* Gaston *he would surely have remained an obscure officer of artillery.)*

General Ulysses Grant . . . *what panache! Led by a* Hiram* *the boys in blue would have cracked;* Gettysburg *would have gone the other way. Under President* Oscar Lincoln *the Union would have been sundered. There would have been no Bicentennial.*

And speaking of panache, one knows that if Rostand had not celebrated Cyrano de Bergerac *but* Adolphe

---

The General did in fact start life as Hiram.

Blanc *he would have flopped in the provinces and never made it to Paris, let alone to immortality.*

The Office of Nomenclature Stabilization was set up in the late 1940s to bring order to this situation. Over the years it has helped countless families on the verge of settling for Dora or Chick, rose fanciers, racehorse breeders, yacht owners, and suburban home builders, and has sent many on their way rejoicing.

To give an idea of the service, our favorite horticulturist is, quite properly, named Flor. Excellent. But pretty girls will be wed. So the Office combed its files, alerted its correspondents, and has short-listed the following suitors: Prof. della Flor, botanist, author of La Nostra Flora; Mr. Bloom, horticulturist, Norfolk, Virginia; Mr. Rose, Head Gardener, Birmingham University School; and Hyacinthe Ringrose, attorney, New York City (among several dozen others). We understand that a selection is being made from these suitable names.

In the following pages, then, anxious parents may see how others have solved the same problems they now confront. The examples, names of actual persons compiled over several decades, are arranged alphabetically by given name. One should look in the Index for one's family name, (e.g. Reuss, on page 35) and then find the suggestions at the pages indicated.

Every source cited (e.g. the New York Times) is in our files and has been verified as carefully as time (and funds!) permit. Any corrections or later information will be gratefully received, together with nominations for the next edition—always, please, with documentation—addressed to *The Office of Nomenclature Stabilization, 345 Park Avenue, New York, New York, 10022. Most undocumented submissions prove to be inaccurate or nonexistent. (Entries in the present text of whose authenticity we are satisfied but on which further information would be welcome are indicated thus: U.S.A.)*

Fifty years ago, contemplating Bible Belt folkways with fascinated dismay, H. L. Mencken* noted many prodigious given names, among which the following stand out: Chlorine, Coita, Dewdrop, Faucette, La Morte, Larceny, La Urine, Margorilla, Mecca, Merdina, Phalla, Twitty, Uretha, *and* Zippa (*female*); *and* Arson, Blasphemy, Blitzkrieg, Bugger, Cad, Constipation, *and* Overy (*male*). Dinette *and* Lotowana *are in the 1933–34 New York* Social Register.

More recent candidates have come forward, however, whose claims are also hard to deny: Buzz Buzz *and* La Void†, *together with* Flourine Thermal *and—from Jamaica—*Little Tits.

From the large but, alas, unverified collection of Mr. George Hubbard of New York we find intriguing Aphrodite Chuckass, Heidi Yum-Yum Gluck, Sexious Boonjug, Sistine Madonna McClung *and* Zita Apathy. *We would welcome verification from our readers.*

---

*Supplement II: The American Language. New York: Alfred A. Knopf, 1948.

†Peter Farb, Word Play. *New York: Alfred A. Knopf, 1974.*

Mrs. Verbal Funderburk (*Lakeland, Florida*) *wrote to our collaborator, Professor William Grierson of the University of Florida, inquiring plaintively if she had the funniest name in the world. Fortunately, our earlier collection had just appeared. He sent his copy to her and her concern was laid to rest.*

Still in Florida, Mr. Everett Williams, Chief of the State's Bureau of Vital Statistics, has become overnight a figure of modest consequence in onomastic circles by releasing several discoveries, the result of many years' transactions of the Bureau, including Mac Aroni *and* Cigar Stubbs, *as well as* Teflon, Lavoris, *and* Truewillinglaughinglifebuckyboomermanifestdestiny *among given names. His position should permit Mr. Williams to perform an important role in the work of the Office, and we urge him on to redoubled efforts.*

As a by-product of détente we are considering an affiliate in the Soviet Union. After the Revolution, optimistic comrades favored names like Tractor *or* Electrification. *One enthusiast called his twin daughters* Anarchy *and* Utopia. *A frequent practice was to contrive such acronyms as* Melsor (Marx-Engels-Lenin-Stalin-October-Revolution).* *Now that the whole business has turned sour and become something one would rather not be reminded of, and with even* Pravda *deploring these "tasteless inventions," the classless parents are at a loss. Authoritative guidance*

A Melsor *recently dropped the S (for Stalin) to become* Melor (Associated Press).

would, we understand, be welcome. We will be there. Our preliminary approved list includes Peaceful Coexistence *and* Virgin Lands *for girls, and for boys,* Norm, SAM, *and* Posthumus Rehabilitation.

Finally, the Office shares with its correspondents its satisfaction at the verification of Dr. Zoltan Ovary, on whom information was sought. Dr. Ovary proves to be a noted gynecologist, now at New York Hospital. Our respects to the Doctor, and, of course, to Madame Ovary.

J. T.

Aristotle Tottle, a very timid feeble pyrate

A. A. A. D'ARTAGNAN UMSLOPAGAAS
DYNAMITE MACAULAY
   (*London Times*)

A. MORON
   Commissioner of Education
   Virgin Islands

ANNE AASS
   Pittsburgh, Pennsylvania

APPENDICITIS, LARYNGITIS, MENINGITIS,
PERITONITIS, and TONSILLITIS JACKSON
   (*Newsweek*)

A. PRZYBYSZ*
   Detroit, Michigan

ARYSTOTLE TOTTLE†
   Pirate
   Falmouth, England

*Changed his name in 1940—to C. Przybysz. (Newsweek)

†"*A timid pyrate.*" Gosse, A History of Piracy. *New York:*
Tudor Publishing Co., 1934.

A. TOXEN WORM
   Theatrical Press Agent
   New York City

AVE MARIA KLINKENBERG
   Yonkers, New York

PRIVATE BABY CHERRY*
   U. S. Army
   (225th Quartermaster Battalion)

BAMBINA BROCCOLI†
   New York City

BASIL CRAPSTER‡
   Princeton University (Class of 1941)
   Princeton, New Jersey

*Compare Private Parts, U.S. Army, and Private Murder
Smith, British Army.

†Compare Concerto Macaroni.

‡Compare E. C. Crapp, Washington, D. C.; Gladstone P.
Lillycrap, U.S. Attorney; and Toilet Jacobs. Sharon Willfahrt
and Tunis Wind were students of the Art Instruction School,
Minneapolis, Minn.

Sir Basil Smallpeice
    Chairman, Cunard Line
    London, England

Bathsheba Finkelstein
    High School of Music & Art (Class of 1957)
    New York City

B. Brooklyn Bridge
    (*John Hancock Life Insurance Company*)

Rev. Blanco White*

Bluey Cole Snow
    (*John Hancock Life Insurance Company*)

Mrs. Belcher Wack Wack†

*A waverer. Ordained a priest in 1800; thereafter Professor of Religion. Renounced Christianity and abandoned the priesthood, 1810. Re-embraced Christianity, 1812; re-ordained, 1814. (Dictionary of National Biography)

†Miss Belcher married Mr. Wack and then married his brother.

BUGLESS, ENERGETIC, EUPHRATES, and
GOLIATH SMITH*
(Indexes of Births for England and Wales)

MESSRS. BULL and SCHYTT
Glaciologists
General Assembly, International Union of
Geodesy and Geophysics
Geneva, Switzerland

BUNCHA LOVE†
(Newsweek)

BUNYAN SNIPES WOMBLE, Lawyer, and
CALDER WELLINGTON WOMBLE‡
Winston-Salem, North Carolina

REVEREND CANAAN BANANA
African National Council
Rhodesia

*Cited in Dunkling, First Names First. London: J. M.
Dent and Sons, 1977

†Compare Felicity Pratt Love, Holy Love, and Wonderful
Love, all of New York. Miss Magnetic Love was a secretary in the
Army Air Corps. Hastie Love was convicted of rape in Tennessee.

‡"He enjoyed discussing the hyphen which in 1913 forever
linked the towns of Winston and Salem," and for which,
indeed, as head of the Winston Consolidation Committee, he was
in large measure responsible.

Buncha Love

Cardinal Sin, Archbishop of Manila

CARBON PETROLEUM DUBBS*
  Founder, Universal Oil Products
  Des Plains, Illinois

CARDINAL SIN
  Archbishop of Manila
  Philippines

CARESSE PECOR
  University of Vermont (Class of 1971)
  Burlington, Vermont

CARLOS RESTREPO RESTREPO RESTREPO
DE RESTREPO
  Medellin, Colombia

REVEREND CHRISTIAN CHURCH†
  Florence, Italy

CIGAR STUBBS
  Florida
  Bureau of Vital Statistics

COL. CLARENCE CLAPSADDLE
  U. S. Army (West Point, Class of 1940)

Also introduced the Japanese beetle to Bermuda.
†*Active in 1966 flood relief effort. Compare Christ Apostle*
and Conception de Jesus, both of New York City, and Rev. God,
of Congaree, S.C.

SIR CLOUDSLEY SHOVEL*
   Admiral, Royal Navy

MR. COCK MARRIED MISS PRICK†
   (*London Times, 1963*)

CRAPPER, LIMITED, TOILETS‡
   London, England

Concluding a distinguished career, he ran the fleet on the rocks (Scilly Isles) in 1707, drowning 2,000 men. After struggling ashore, he was done in by a peasant woman who "coveted an emerald ring on one of his fingers, and extinguished his flickering life." He was buried in Westminster Abbey, "where an elaborate monument in very questionable taste was erected to his memory." (Dictionary of National Biography) His gallant successor Admiral The Hon. Sir Reginald Aylmer Ranfurley Plunkett-Ernle-Erle-Drax participated in the Battle of Jutland. Captain Strong Boozer commanded the Guantanamo Naval Base, but Royal Naval Shippe has opted for life ashore with the Federal Reserve System, Washington, D.C.

†*A Mr. Ora Jones married a Miss Ora Jones in 1941.* (R. L. Ripley)

‡*Thomas Crapper's biography is aptly titled* Flushed With Pride.

Sir Cloudesley Shovel, Admiral, Royal Navy

Cumming & Gooing, Louisiana

CUMMING & GOOING
    Louisiana
    (*New Yorker*)

DAPHNE READER'S DIGEST TAIONE
    Utui, Vavao, Tonga

DEFRED GOO FOLTS
    Director of Placement
    Harvard Graduate School of Business
    Administration
    Cambridge, Massachusetts

DOCTOR DOCTOR*
    (*American Medical Directory*)

There were, by recent count, 13 doctors Doctor, Docter, or Doktor in the U.S.; 5 doctors Bonebreak; 1 Bonecutter; 18 Butchers; several Cutters and Carvers; 184 Paines or Paynes and 11 Pangs. Dr. Bonesetter practices in Bombay, and Dr. Fillerup in Pasadena, Calif. as an obstetrician. Dr. Screech practices in Victoria, British Columbia, and another Dr. Screech is a dentist in Essex, England. For Dr. Ovary, gynecologist, vide supra, p. 62. Among the Mormons, the seventh son of a seventh son may be named Doctor. W. Doctor Dollar, New York, has not yet entered the profession, but should.

D. Schumuk, Political Activist, Ukraine

D. SCHUMUK*
    Political Activist
    Ukraine, U. S. S. R.
    (*Reuters*)

EPAPHRODITUS MARSH
ONESIPHORUS MARSH and
(ARCHBISHOP) NARCISSUS MARSH
    (*New York Times*)

FANNY FINGER†
    New York City

A loser. Served 7 years in jail (prewar) for communism. Then (postwar) served 20 years and in 1972 started an additional 10 years plus 5 years exile, all for anti-communism.

†*Compare Hyman Peckeroff, taxi driver, New York City; and Hyman Pleasure, Assistant Commissioner, New York State Department of Mental Hygiene.*

CHARLES ADOLPHE FAUX-PAS BIDET*
  Commissaire de Police
  Paris, France

F. G. VERENESENECKOCKKROCKOFF†
  San Francisco, California

FIRMIN A. GRYP
  Banker
  Northern California Savings & Loan
  Association
  Palo Alto, California

(MADAME) FOUQUEAU DE PUSSY‡
  Authoress

*The Sûreté's ace on Russian intrigues, Faux-Pas Bidet
received heavy press coverage in the 1930s when he investigated
the abduction of Gen. Kutylpov, a White Russian leader in
Paris. The general was seized in the street by OGPU agents
and apparently, wrapped up as merchandise, was carried on
board a Soviet ship, the* Spartak, *which immediately put out
to sea.*

†*Defendant in a celebrated murder trial in 1897. See*
Jennings, Personalities of Language. *London: Gollancz, 1967.*

‡Le Grand-père et ses quatre petits fils. *Boston:
Hickling, Swan and Brown, 1855. Compare Graze Pussy,
New York City.*

Madame Fouqueau de Pussy, Authoress

MRS. FRIENDLY LEY*
  Mission Hills, California

BARONESS GABY VON BAGGE OF BOO
  (*New York Times*)

GASTON J. FEEBLEBUNNY
  U. S. A.

GEORGE BARETITS
  U. S. Army

GISELLA WERBEZIRK-PIFFL†
  Actress
  Vienna and Hollywood

On whose career of amiability the curtain descended when her husband's revolver, which he was cleaning in the kitchen, went off.

†*Perennial victim of prewar Hollywood jokers who liked to telephone from poolside to ask if she was the Gisella Werbezirk-Piffl they had met in (e.g.) Monte Carlo the previous summer; on receiving assurance to the contrary they would pronounce grandly, "Ah! Then that must have been another Gisella Werbezirk-Piffl!" Compare Josette Legg Snowball (Actress, D'Oyly Carte Company).*

Mrs Friendly Ley, Mission Hills, California

HEINRICH LXXIV

Prince Heinrich the Seventy-Fourth of Reuss, Thuringia, Germany

GRECIAN T. SNOOZE*
　　Australian University Student (Class of 1950)

GROANER DIGGER†
　　Undertaker
　　Houston, Texas
　　(*Today's Health*)

HALLOWEEN BUGGAGE
　　The Charity Hospital
　　New Orleans, Louisiana

PRINCE HEINRICH THE 74TH OF REUSS‡
　　Jankendorf, Germany

HORACINE CLUTCH
　　Pelham, New York

*Dunkling, op. cit.

†*Compare Goody P. Creep, Undertaker. The Quick-Park Funeral Home may be found at 617 Columbus Avenue, Sandusky.*

‡*Born 1798. Since 1693 all males in this ancient family have been named Heinrich.*

(Miss) Horsey de Horsey*
    Intimate friend of Lord Cardigan†

Hrothgar J. Habakkuk
    Vice-Chancellor, Oxford University
    Oxford, England

Hugh Pugh
    Landscape Architect
    London, England

Humperdink Fangboner‡
    Lumber Dealer, and
    Fanny Fangboner
    Nurse
    Sandusky, Ohio

I. C. Shivers
    Iceman
    (*John Hancock Life Insurance Company*)

Compare The Honorable Outerbridge Horsey, U.S. Ambassador to Czechoslovakia.

†*Who on a notable occasion banged on her door shouting, "My dearest, she's dead!"—referring to her late Ladyship— "Let's get married at once!"*

‡*Folks in Sandusky, as in some towns in Oklahoma, seem to feel better having odd names. Other citizens of the area include Ovid Futch, Xenophon Hassenpflug, Kitty Ditty, and (from the Sandusky Register) E. Kickapoo Banfill, Lecturer.*

Miss Horsey de Horsey

IMA and URA HOGG
　　Social Leaders
　　Houston, Texas

IONA VICTORY BOND
　　Victoria, British Columbia

I. O. SILVER
　　(*Philadelphia Evening Bulletin*)

I. P. FRILLI*
　　Master Mechanic
　　Florence, Italy

IRIS FAIRCLOTH BLITCH
　　Congresswoman
　　Washington, D. C.

JOHN SENIOR, JUNIOR†
　　New York City

---

*Compare P. P. Fast, Fla., Mrs. Tiney Sprinkle, New York
City, and Tom Passwater, Art Instruction School,
Minneapolis, Minn. A Mr. Uren changed his name to Wren
(1897)—understandably.*

†*Who must bear partial responsibility for that deplorable
nuisance, New York Airways.*

JOY BANG
  Actress
  New York City

JULY AUGUST SEPTEMBER
  (*Today's Health*)

JUSTIN TUNE
  Chorister
  Westminster Choir College (Class of 1947)
  Princeton, New Jersey

KATZ MEOW
  Hoquiam, Washington
  (*Collier's*)

KATZ PAJAMA COMPANY*
  New York City

*Compare Climax Underwear Co., Cincinnati, O.

Katz Meow, Hoquiam, Washington

LARRY DERRYBERRY*
  Attorney General
  Oklahoma City, Oklahoma

LAVENDER SIDEBOTTOM†
  Masseuse, Elizabeth Arden
  New York City

LAWLESS & LYNCH
  Attorneys
  Jamaica, New York

LETTICE GOEDEBED
  Johannesburg, South Africa

LINUS KLUEMPER‡
  Jasper, Indiana

Also Harry Derryberry, Lima, O., and Jerry Derryberry, Chattanooga, Tenn.

†N. b.: Epitaph of Mr. Longbottom, who died young: Arse longa, vita brevis.*

‡Attained celebrity in August 1955 when a fan in his bedroom window wriggled five feet toward him and chopped off the big toe of his right foot.*

LOUIS GEORGE MAURICE ADOLPH
ROCH ALBERT ABEL ANTONIO
ALEXANDRE NOÉ JEAN LUCIEN
DANIEL EUGENÈ JOSEPH-LE-BRUN
JOSEPHE-BARÊME THOMAS THOMAS THOMAS-
THOMAS PIERRE ARBON PIERRE-MAUREL
BARTHELEMI ARTUS ALPHONSE BERTRAND
DIEUDONNÉ EMANUEL JOSUÉ VINCENT
LUC MICHEL JULES-DE-LA-PLANE JULES-
BAZIN JULIO CESAR JULLIEN*
    Orchestra Conductor
    Sisteron, France

LOYAL LODGE NO. 296 KNIGHTS OF
PYTHIAS PONCA CITY OKLAHOMA SMITH†
    Ponca City, Oklahoma

LUSCIOUS PEA
    The Charity Hospital
    New Orleans, Louisiana

*Born in 1812, the Maestro was for obvious reasons known
simply as The Conductor Jullien. On June 15, 1854, he presented
The Firemen's Quadrille in the Crystal Palace in New York.
At the climax, by prearrangement, flames burst out, engine
bells rang in the streets, the windows were broken and firemen
burst in spewing water from their hoses. Dozens of spectators
collapsed as others fought to leave the hall. Jullien died, insane,
in 1856.

†Born August 21, 1876. Mencken, op. cit.

LYULPH YDWALLO ODIN NESTOR EGBERT
LYONEL TOEDMAG HUGH ERCHENWYNE
SAXON ESA CROMWELL ORMA NEVILL
DYSART PLANTAGENET TOLLEMACHE-
TOLLEMACHE
  Bentleigh, Otumoetai,
  Tauranga, New Zealand
  (*Burke's Peerage and Baronetage*)

MADONNA GHOSTLY
  Teacher
  Washington, D.C.

MRS. MAGINIS OYSTER
  Social Leader
  San Rafael, California
  (*Social Register*)

MAJOR MINOR
  U.S. Army

MARK CLARK VAN ARK
  Toledo, Ohio

Mary Maloof Teabaggy, Boston

MARY LOUISE PANTZAROFF*
    Huron County, Ohio

MELISSY DALCINY CALDONY YANKEE
PANKEE DEVIL-TAKE-THE-IRISHMAN GARRISON
    Tryon City, North Carolina

(MISS) MEMORY LANE
    Roslyn High School, New York

MENE MENE TEKEL UPHARSIN POND
    Hartford, Connecticut

MERCY BUMPUS†
    Wife of "General Tom Thumb"

MOO, BOO, GOO, and LITTLE MISS MAY
    New Orleans, Louisiana

MOON UNIT ZAPPA and DWEEZLE ZAPPA
    Hollywood, California

*Compare Mary Maloof Teabaggy, Boston, Mass.

†Enjoyed the specialized distinction of being fought over by
the General and his tiny rival, Commodore Nutt.

Mustafa Kunt*
    Turkish Military Attaché
    Moscow, U. S. S. R.

Newton Hooton
    Cambridge, Massachusetts

N. Guppy†
    The Pond, Haddenham
    Cambridge, England

Nita Bath
    (*Philadelphia Evening Bulletin*)

Noble Teat‡
    Still Pond, Maryland

*Occasion of much ribald official cable traffic, along with his vis-à-vis, Major R. Rectanus, U.S. Assistant Military Attaché, Moscow. Of Gen. Plastiras (Greece) Winston Churchill expressed the hope that he did not have "feet of clay."

†The fish is named for the family, not vice versa.

‡Compare Faithful Teate, Dublin "who wrote a quaint poem on the Trinity." (Encyclopedia Britannica)

Norman Icenoggle
  (*Associated Press*)

Odile, Odelia, Olive, Oliver,
Olivia, Ophelia, Odelin, Octave,
Octavia, Ovide, Onesia, Olite, Otto,
Ormes, and Opta Maynard*
    Abbeville, Louisiana

O. Hell
    Contractor
    Alto Adige, Italy

Ophelia Legg
    Norwalk, Ohio

Orange Marmalade Lemon
    Wichita, Kansas

Original Bug
    Liverpool, England
    (*Liverpool Echo*)

Dunkling, op. cit.

Original Bug, Liverpool

OSBORN OUTHOUSE
  Boston, Massachusetts

PENINNAH SWINGLE HOGENCAMP UMBACH
  Spiritualist Minister
  Charleston, South Carolina

MISS PENSIVE COCKE*
  Secretary
  U. S. Army Air Corps

MISS PINKEY DICKEY DUKES
  Branchville, South Carolina

*Compare Mrs. Seeman Glasscock; J. Badcock, Editor, London; B. Grocock, Teacher, Washington, D.C.; D. Grewcock, Stockbroker, N.Y.; and the Griesedieck (beer) family of St. Louis. The Koch Erecting Company is a major supplier to New York City, while the Dicke Tool Company operates in Bronxville, N.Y. Cinderella Hardcock and D. Biggerdick studied with the Art Instruction School, Minneapolis. Respectful attention is bestowed on the good Cornish family of Trebilcock and concerned awareness on Prof. A. O. J. Cockshut. W. J. Uglow Woolcock appears in Boyle's Court Guide for 1915. Cf. P. H. Reaney, The Origin of English Surnames. London: Routledge and Kegan Paul, 1967, p. 209 et seq.

PLATO FOUFAS
   Real Estate
   Chicago, Illinois

PLUMMER & LEEK
   Plumbers
   Sheringham, Norfolk
   (*London Times*)

POSITIVE WASSERMANN JOHNSON*
   Evanston, Illinois

PRESERVED FISH, JR.†
   New Bedford, Massachusetts

PRIMROSE GOO
   Hawaii

RAPID INTEGRATION
   (*Newsweek*)

---

*"*Probably represents the indelicate humor of a medical student.*"—H. L. Mencken, The American Language, *Fourth Edition, New York: Alfred A. Knopf, 1936.*

†*Born in 1766; partner in firm said to market whale oil in two grades: "good and bad." His father and other forebears bore the same name. "There is no foundation to the oft repeated story that his name was bestowed by a New Bedford fisherman who found him as an infant adrift at sea in an open boat."* (Dictionary of American Biography)

Preserved Fish, Jr.

Ronald Supena
    Lawyer
    (*Philadelphia Evening Bulletin*)

Rosebud Rosenbloom
    Ethical Culture School
    New York City

Rosetta Stone
    New York City

Salome Casanova
    Havana, Cuba and Madrid, Spain

Santiago Nudelman
    Publisher
    Brazil

Mrs. Screech
    Singing Teacher
    Victoria, British Columbia

Shanda Lear*
    Battle Creek, Michigan

Of the Lear Jet Lears.

SHINE SOON SUN*
    Geophysicist
    Houston, Texas

SIDDHARTHA GREENBLATT
    (*Harper's Magazine*)

SILENCE BELLOWS†
    Editor
    (*Christian Science Monitor*)

SODAWATER BOTTLEWALLA
    Bombay, India
    (*New York Times*)

STRANGEWAYS PIGG STRANGEWAYS
    Cricket Star
    London, England

SUPARPORN POOPATTANA
    New York City

*Compare Moon Bong Kang, Korean Ambassador to Switzerland.

†*Vermont Connecticut Royster is editor of the other reliable American paper, the* Wall Street Journal.

Lt. Gen. H.H. Shri Shri Shri (etc... 108 times)
Maharajadhiraj, the Maharega of Patiala

LT. GEN. HIS HIGHNESS SHRI SHRI SHRI
SHRI SHRI SHRI SHRI SHRI SHRI SHRI
SHRI SHRI SHRI SHRI SHRI SHRI SHRI
SHRI SHRI SHRI SHRI SHRI SHRI SHRI
SHRI SHRI SHRI SHRI SHRI SHRI SHRI
SHRI SHRI SHRI SHRI SHRI SHRI SHRI
SHRI SHRI SHRI SHRI SHRI SHRI SHRI
SHRI SHRI SHRI SHRI SHRI SHRI SHRI
SHRI SHRI SHRI SHRI SHRI SHRI SHRI
SHRI SHRI SHRI SHRI SHRI SHRI SHRI
SHRI SHRI SHRI SHRI SHRI SHRI SHRI
SHRI SHRI SHRI SHRI SHRI SHRI SHRI
SHRI SHRI SHRI SHRI SHRI SHRI SHRI
SHRI SHRI SHRI SHRI SHRI SHRI SHRI
SHRI SHRI SHRI SHRI SHRI SHRI SHRI
SHRI SHRI SHRI SHRI SHRI SHRI SHRI
MAHARAJADHIRAJ RAJ RAJESHWAR
SHRI MAHARJA-I-RAJGAN MARARAJA
SIR YADVINDRA SINGH MAHENDRA
BAHADUR, YADU VANSHAVATANS BHATTI
KUL BHUSHAN RAJPRAMUKH OF PATIALA*
India and London, England

*Born in 1913, the Maharaja of Patiala is also the leader of
the Sikh community, all of whose members bear the surname
Singh (meaning lion). The sequence in the first part of the
title is usually contracted to "Shri 108."

Supply Clapp Thwing
  Harvard College (Class of 1837)

Mrs. Tackaberry McAdoo
  Social Leader
  New York City
  (*Social Register*)

Tetley Ironside Tetley Jones
  Chairman, Tetley Tea Company
  London, England

T. Hee
  Restaurant Employee
  New York City

Thusnelda Neusbickle
  Wellesley College
  Wellesley, Massachusetts

Trailing Arbutus Vines*
  Cumberland Mountains, Tennessee

Ufuk Restaurant
  Izmir, Turkey

Mencken, op. cit.

Ufuk Restaurant, Izmir, Turkey.

UNABLE TO FORNICATE*
    Indian Chief
    Northwestern U. S.

MRS. V. D. WHYNOT†
    U. S. A.

MR. VENUS BONAPARTE
    (*London Times*)

VERBAL FUNDERBURK
    Lakeland, Florida

MR. VICE‡
    Malefactor
    New Orleans, Louisiana

VIRGINIA MAY SWEATT STRONG
    Memphis, Tennessee

Reported by Mencken. Fly-Fornication was a good Puritan name.

†*Linda Whynot was convicted of lewd and wanton behavior in the Gemini Hotel, Providence, R.I.* (Providence Journal)

‡*Arrested 820 times and convicted 421, probably a record.* (International Herald Tribune)

Mr. Vice, Malefactor, New Orleans

VIOLET ORGAN*
   Art Historian
   New York City

VOLUME DINGLE†
   Tampa, Florida

MR. VROOM‡
   Motorcycle Dealer
   Port Elizabeth, South Africa
   (*New York Times*)

WARREN PEACE
   Williams College, Massachusetts

SIR W. C. DAMPIER-WHETHAM
   Upwater Lodge, Cambridge

WELCOME BABY DARLING
   Greenwich, Connecticut

Biographer of the American painter Robert Henri. She never married. Compare Violet Butt, Washington, D.C., and Noble Butt, Boston.

†*His wife threw out his pants, containing his life's savings.* (Tampa Tribune)

‡*Compare Joy Auto Collision, Toronto, and Fuzle-Rub Motor Training School, Calcutta.*

Mr Vroom, Motorcycle Dealer, Port Elizabeth,
South Africa

WILLIAM MCKINLEY LOUISIANA
LEVEEBUST SMITH*
　　Richmond, Virginia

WYRE & TAPPING†
　　Detectives
　　New York City

YELBERTON ABRAHAM TITTLE
　　Quarterback, New York Giants
　　New York City

ZEZOZOSE ZADFRACK‡
　　California

ZODA VIOLA KLONTZ GAZOLA
　　U. S. A.

DR. ZOLTAN OVARY
　　Gynecologist, New York Hospital
　　New York City

*Mencken, op. cit.

†*The Office of Nomenclature Stabilization has a photograph of this establishment.*

‡*Natural son of C. Manson, Mass Murderer, by a Miss Atkins.*

INDEX OF FAMILY NAMES